Complete Variations
for Solo Piano

Ludwig van Beethoven

Complete Variations
for Solo Piano

———

Dover Publications, Inc.
New York

Published in Canada by General Publishing Company, Ltd., 30 Lesmill Road, Don Mills, Toronto, Ontario.
Published in the United Kingdom by Constable and Company, Ltd.

This Dover edition, first published in 1986, is an unabridged republication, in altered sequence of pieces, of "Serie 17. Variationen für das Pianoforte" from *Ludwig van Beethoven's Werke. Vollständige kritisch durchgesehene überall berechtigte Ausgabe. Mit Genehmigung aller Originalverleger,* as originally published by Breitkopf & Härtel, Leipzig (complete set, 1862–1865).

Manufactured in the United States of America
Dover Publications, Inc., 31 East 2nd Street, Mineola, N.Y. 11501

Library of Congress Cataloging-in-Publication Data

Beethoven, Ludwig van, 1770–1827.
  [Variations, piano]
  Complete variations for solo piano.

  Reprint. Originally published: Leipzig : Breitkopf & Härtel, ca. 1864 (Ludwig van Beethoven's Werke ; Ser. 17)
  1. Variations (Piano) I. Title.
M27.B   86-752130
ISBN 0-486-25188-8 (pbk.)

Contents

The present Dover volume follows the chronological sequence established by Douglas Johnson in the article on Beethoven in *The New Grove Dictionary of Music and Musicians* (1980). The last piece in the volume (with asterisk), which appears in the original Breitkopf & Härtel edition but is not listed in *Grove*, is included here for the sake of completeness.

Complete Variations
for Solo Piano

———

Nine Variations
on a March by Dressler, WoO 63

1

VAR. VI.

Nine Variations on a March by Dressler

Nine Variations on a March by Dressler

24 Variations
on an Arietta by Righini, WoO 65

VAR.III.

VAR.IV.

attacca subito l' Allegro

13 Variations
on an Arietta by Dittersdorf, WoO 66

VAR. I.

VAR. II.

VAR. X.

13 Variations on an Arietta by Dittersdorf

Capriccio.
Andante.

Six Easy Variations
on a Swiss Song, WoO 64

Six Easy Variations on a Swiss Song

12 Variations
on a Theme by Haibel, WoO 68

12 Variations on a Theme by Haibel

VAR.X.

VAR.XI.

VAR.XII.

Allegro.

a tempo.

Nine Variations
on an Aria by Paisiello, WoO 69

Nine Variations on an Aria by Paisiello

VAR.VI.

VAR.VII.

Six Variations
on a Duet by Paisiello, WoO 70

VAR.III.

VAR.IV.

VAR.V.

Eight Variations
on a Romance by Grétry, WoO 72

VAR. VII.

Allegro.

VAR. VIII.

12 Variations
on a Dance by Wranitzky, WoO 71

12 Variations on a Dance by Wranitzky

VAR. V.

VAR. VI.

Maggiore.

VAR. VIII.

VAR. IX.

Ten Variations
on a Duet by Salieri, WoO 73

VAR. VII.

VAR. VIII.

p dolce

88   *Ten Variations on a Duet by Salieri*

90   *Ten Variations on a Duet by Salieri*

Ten Variations on a Duet by Salieri

Eight Variations
on a Trio by Süssmayr, WoO 76

Eight Variations on a Trio by Süssmayr

VAR. IV.

Eight Variations on a Trio by Süssmayr

Eight Variations on a Trio by Süssmayr

Seven Variations
on a Quartet by Winter, WoO 75

VAR. I.

VAR. III.

VAR. IV.

Seven Variations on a Quartet by Winter

Seven Variations on a Quartet by Winter

Coda.

Allegro molto.

Six Easy Variations
on an Original Theme, WoO 77

Six Easy Variations on an Original Theme

Six Variations
on an Original Theme, Op. 34

VAR. I.

Tempo di Menuetto.

VAR. IV.

Six Variations on an Original Theme, Op. 34

VAR.VI. Allegretto.

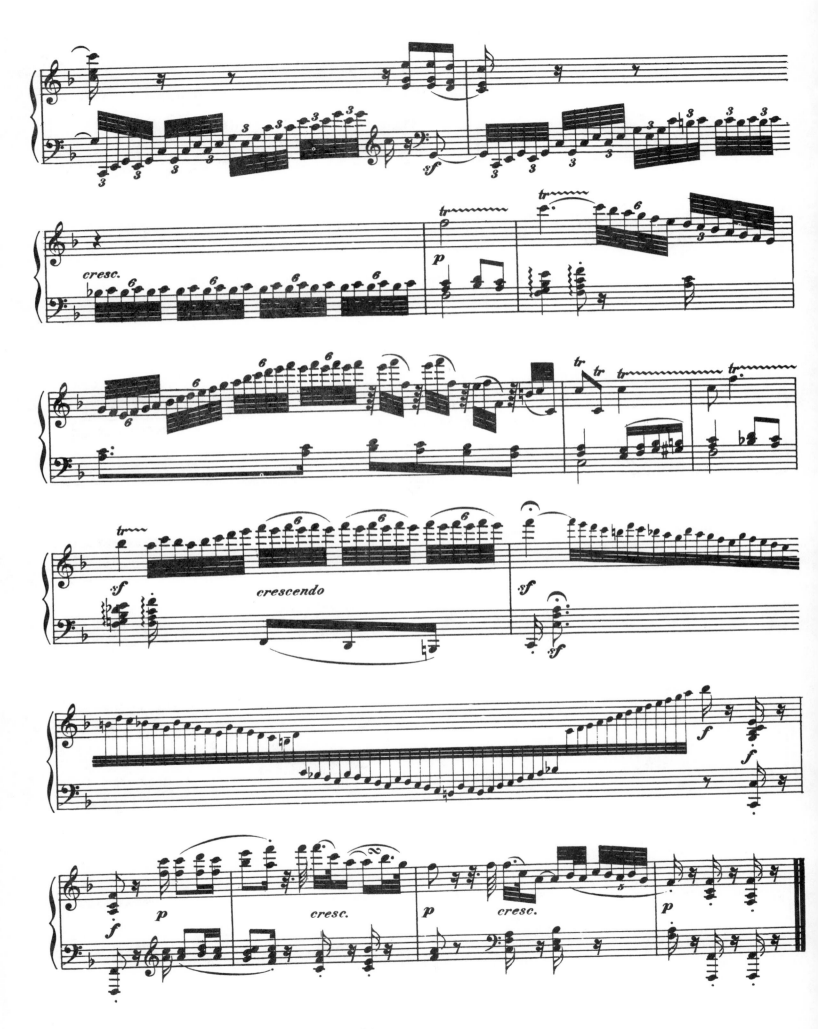

Six Variations on an Original Theme, Op. 34

15 Variations and Fugue
on an Original Theme ("Eroica Variations"), Op. 35

Canone all'ottava.

VAR. VII.

VAR. VIII.

"Eroica Variations"

"Eroica Variations"

"Eroica Variations"

Seven Variations
on "God Save the King," WoO 78

Seven Variations on "God Save the King"

Seven Variations on "God Save the King"

Five Variations
on "Rule Britannia," WoO 79

Five Variations on "Rule Britannia"

VAR. II.

sempre legato

VAR. III.

Five Variations on "Rule Britannia"

32 Variations
on an Original Theme, WoO 80

32 Variations on an Original Theme

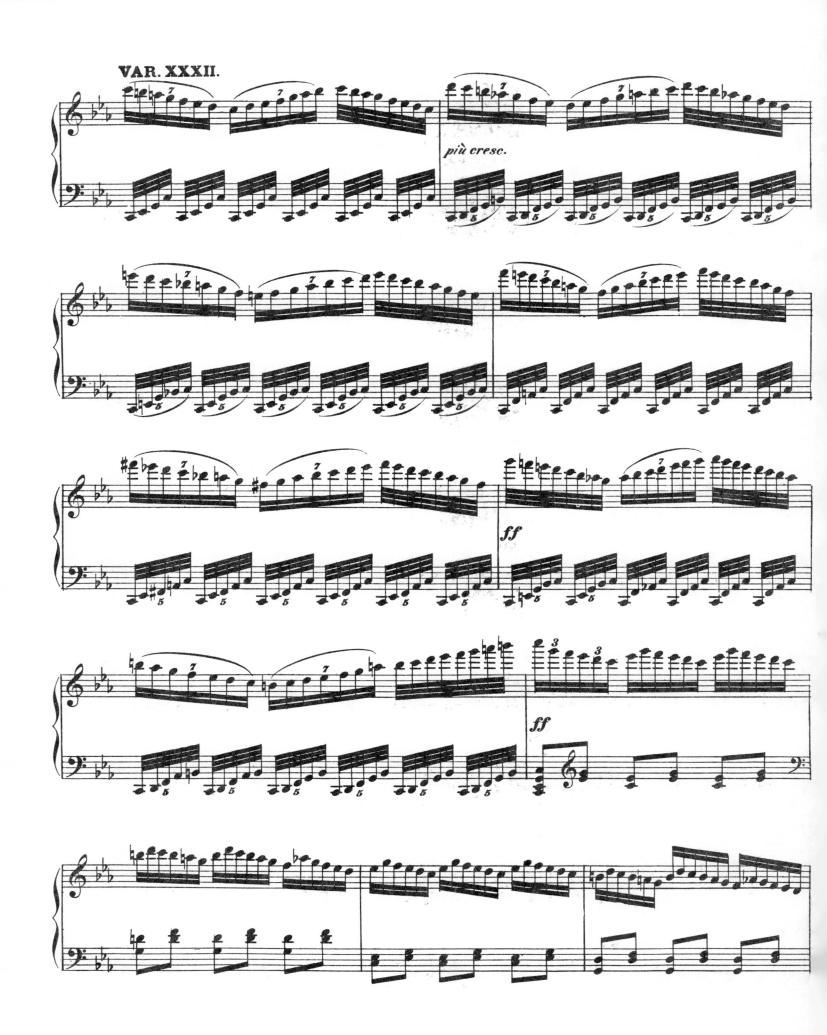

Six Variations
on an Original Theme, Op. 76

VAR. IV.

33 Variations
on a Waltz by Diabelli, Op. 120

Un poco più allegro.

VAR.VII.

33 Variations on a Waltz by Diabelli

33 Variations on a Waltz by Diabelli

33 Variations on a Waltz by Diabelli

VAR.XXI.

Allegro con brio.

Meno allegro.

Tempo I.

Meno allegro.

33 Variations on a Waltz by Diabelli

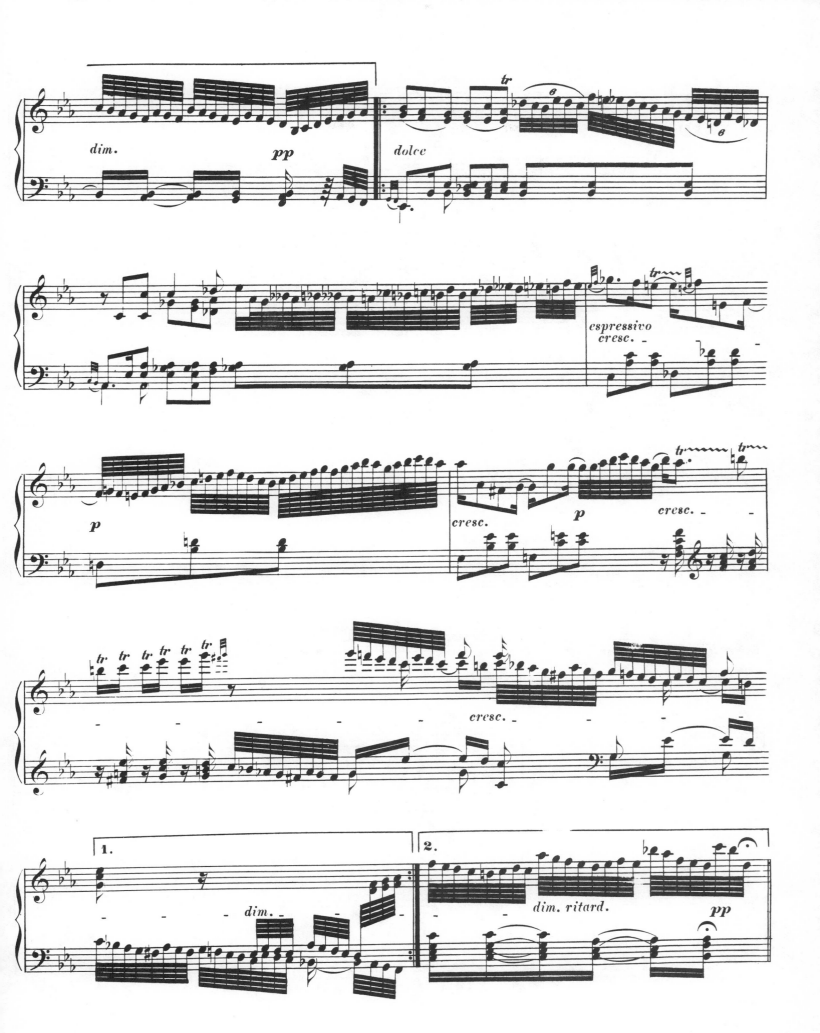

33 Variations on a Waltz by Diabelli

Tempo di Minuetto moderato (ma non tirarsi dietro.)(aber nicht schleppend.)

VAR. XXXIII.

p grazioso e dolce

33 Variations on a Waltz by Diabelli

Eight Variations
on "Ich hab ein kleines Hüttchen nur"

VAR. II.

VAR. III.

Eight Variations on "Ich hab ein kleines Hüttchen nur"

VAR. V.

VAR. VI.

226 *Eight Variations on "Ich hab ein kleines Hüttchen nur"*

Eight Variations on "Ich hab ein kleines Hüttchen nur"